In No Hurry

In No Hurry

Poems by

Michael Carrino

Cover design by Shay Culligan

ISBN: 978-1-954353-77-0

Kelsay Books
502 South 1040 East, A-119
American Fork, Utah, 84003
Kelsaybooks.com

For Thel

and in memory of
Luciana Ricciutelli and Timothy Hartnett

Acknowledgments

The author wishes to acknowledge the editors of the following publications in which these poems appeared:

The American Journal of Poetry: "Touch," "The Piano Tuner of Hiroshima"

Blueline Magazine: "Moonlight," "Winter in Clinton County," "The Magician Who Lives One Flight Above," "In His Lifetime of Tea and Moonlight"

Carolina Quarterly: "Before the Deluge," "Beneath the Queen Elizabeth Hotel"

Conestoga Zen: "The Cricket"

Delmarva Review: "Kokura Luck," "Elm Trees," "Autumn Morning," "In the Summer Afternoon Sky"

Hamilton Stone Review: "Rain," "The Beach House in Autumn"

The Iowa Source: "Crow in Sakura Tree" (in a slightly different version)

J Journal: "The Standing Boy of Nagasaki"

Juniper: "When You Wake After a Storm"

Prole: "Allure"

The RavensPerch: "Again in Autumn," "Bristlecone Pines," "Saw Whet Owl," "The Village"

Speckled Trout Review: "Well Past Midnight as the Pandemic Continues"

Third Wednesday Magazine: "Elderly," " C.W. Pencil Enterprise"

The Tower Journal: "The Field of All Possibilities"

Contents

Touch   13
The Piano Tuner of Hiroshima   14
Kokura Luck   15
The Standing Boy of Nagasaki   16
Crow in Sakura Tree   17
Well Past Midnight as the Pandemic Continues   18
Bristlecone Pines   20
In His Lifetime of Tea and Moonlight   21
Saw Whet Owl   22
Winter in Clinton County   23
Moonlight   24
The Village   25
Allure   26
The Magician Who Lives One Flight Above   27
Before the Deluge   28
Beneath the Queen Elizabeth Hotel   29
When You Wake After a Storm   30
In the Summer Afternoon Sky   31
Elderly   32
The Field of All Possibilities   33
The Cricket   34
Again in Autumn   35
Autumn Morning   36
The Garden of Kyoto   37
Elm Trees   38
Rain   39
The Beach House in Autumn   40
C.W. Pencil Enterprise   41

...I opened myself to the gentle indifference of the world.
—Albert Camus

Touch

There are children on the playground
at Kongevejens Skole outside of Copenhagen
this Wednesday, each delicate voice alive
at recess in a spirited game of tag

without touch. Each child
steps on another child's shadow.

The virus will end, may start
again, but the children want "to really learn in school,"
wash their hands, wash them again and again
as they all wear a mask, step

on one shadow and another. They shriek with glee
content with something familiar, something new.

The Piano Tuner of Hiroshima

Long after that August morning of black rain, blistering
heat, and red sky, Mitsunori Yagawa, born
to hibakusha parents and over time
known to restore, to tune instruments, found many hibakusha
willing to donate a piano, their survivor of the blast. Owners often
wept as if parting from a family member.
Their willingness was due to the artisan Yagawa's passion
to rescue soothing reveries of music, hopeful

that long after the blast, after painstaking restoration
of destruction—glass shards, scarred wood, a charred ruler
that had pierced one piano, Mitsunori Yagawa could restore
some pleasing notes and tones. Yagawa made six Hiroshima pianos
musical again, their echo eased out of shadow into light
when played at peace memorials, schools, hospitals, where
anyone listening might imagine
each piano's melodic plea without words.

Kokura Luck

On that August morning there was never one rupture
in the overcast sky, any rend in lingering
smoke from firebombing raids.
There was a change. Fly south instead
to Nagasaki and some chance
there might be a break in the clouds.

Long after that morning, any brush with misfortune
that might pause, touch anyone,
but swiftly dissolve, leave a chill
on a face, speck of soot in one eye, a shiver
hinting at quake, or disease, any
disaster avoided, was called "Kokura Luck."

Perhaps luck is any well-made plan. Fine outcomes
born of hard labor. Until it is not.
Instead, luck might be a willful, or careless act
when ordinary care
might change everything.
    Imagine Kokura Luck in quiet stillness

between one deep breath, its long
release into that morning   when there was not
one cut in the dark sky.

The Standing Boy of Nagasaki

"Years later, many years later, the nightmares began…"
—Joe O'Donnell, military photographer of the occupation forces

At the edge of the cremation pit
the boy waits as if

at attention for men in white
to loosen the rope

that binds his lifeless
infant brother to his back.

The boy stares into smoke and ash,
his eyes reveal
what anyone might imagine—

how far, how long
this journey, the heat

of that pit. The boy
turning, then walking away.

What might happen
later. Any bearable aftermath.

Crow in Sakura Tree

Tokyo Rainy Season

Glistening onyx, perched on a wet branch
not yet inspired

to extend its wings, impulse mute, quivering
in a pause, prior to another

inevitable day of rain.

Well Past Midnight as the Pandemic Continues

I'm watching the film noir, *Out of the Past,* waiting
for Robert Mitchum to find Jane Greer ease
out of sunlight into a dim, dingy bar, that moment
when their fate is decided. I always watch
how this end plays out. Lately I watch
this film again and again.   I'm tired and close my eyes—
find my brother in New York City at last
finished with his quarantine, walking again every

morning in Greenwich Village, until he reaches
the Hudson, rests on a bench, listening for what is missing
in New York, that break, that improvisation
ingrained in him, so that too much
silence makes any bird song feel ominous
since the virus.   For no fathomable reason
I recall a letter from my father
I kept, but have now

somehow lost. Ten pages of cursive writing, written
after the wake for Rose, my mother's sister. The family
caused some ruckus, came close to being thrown
out of the funeral parlor.   Lush with images, the letter
was so bitingly funny I could barely
catch my breath from laughing as I read it.
Maybe it is an acceptable way to die, choking
while laughing. Only dying asleep

could likely be better, or when viewing *Out of the Past*
without any distraction. My father
favored westerns starring Tom Mix. A cornucopia
of high plains, canyons, and arroyos.   It was romance
for my mother—desire ripe with unforeseen circumstance,

films like *Brief Encounter.* No need for a pandemic
to have the passionate tumble and flail
when life must shift and slant them sideways.

Out of the Past is somehow over. I missed that scene—
sunlight to shadow. My brother remains available
on that bench beside the Hudson. He loves *Juliet of the Spirits,*
all Fellini's surreal, embellished memories. In my reverie
my brother will refuse to consider fever
ever returning or lingering. He will wait for every
sway, refrain, and wail, every
melodic pulse of New York   where he lives.

Bristlecone Pines

"They have the look of survivors, not conquerors."
                                        —Alex Ross

They must be the oldest trees
on earth. Found on the eastern slopes of California's
White Mountains, also along the Wasatch
range in Utah, everywhere contorted and wraithlike
they appear dead but live,
some, five thousand years, or more
it's confirmed when their rings are carefully
examined. The mangled wood
hide a trove of ancient stories. Bristlecones cling

to life, fossil and ribbons of live
bark, each different, acquiring the elderly
appearance of individuals, their dreams, anxieties
projected on and around them, as if joined
and shaped by ice sharp salt, driftwood
from an imagined ocean. Bristlecones
have been called elders, sages and it's true
artists conjure ghosts out of Bristlecones'
writhing shapes, find what
was, what will be, our
blurry, reckless future.

In His Lifetime of Tea and Moonlight

youth had its drama   no time and nothing   but time
each restless hour

now bitter winter indoors   stirs warm reveries
long regrets can fade

no longer young   past   future   become one blue stone
easier to grasp

he sips white tea in a present moment   tranquil
pause in full moonlight

Saw Whet Owl

In evergreens the Saw Whet will roost at eye level
close to the trunk. The size of a robin,
it is hard to find in any Northeastern
forest. Nocturnal, it will feast
on large insects, mice, shrews, voles, even
young squirrels. When found in the Rockefeller Center
Norway Spruce, after a long haul from Oneonta,
it made the evening news, every New York paper.
Three days on the road, no food or water,
an upbeat story amid warnings
of a pandemic surge and approaching
winter. But only good news if that Saw Whet
could survive. It did. It was set free.
　　I've never seen one Saw Whet, in city or forest, given
I don't venture into the wild. I find it hard
to believe owls are some harbinger of death.
If they are, I can only imagine owls
far down any grim list.
　　I hope anyone will find the satisfaction
they desire, at least one small
object of even some unquestionable need.
　　Tonight I will imagine
the Saw Whet owl of Rockefeller Center
in an evergreen forest. Alive.
　　Safe in the present moment.

Winter in Clinton County

Last of the curling leaves scatter crisp across
the lake beach touched by wind that hints

at winter shadows   last summer now far
gone   snow and below zero soon

what stuns me always is how
winter can quickly have me

forget the turn of season   spring far off
hard to imagine another fall

another summer as each stone-gray day
makes short work of daylight

has me conjuring
        one more leaving

Moonlight

full and pagan white
    watch it

sparkle Lake Champlain's
    thick ice

curl this vibrant night
    silent

undeniably

    patient

The Village

There are bare maples and one narrow dirt road
slick with fresh snow. Morning

light is changing, granite to ice blue. In curling
chimney smoke there is no hint

winter might be less harsh, or that spring will
arrive here early.

Allure

That back road must be slick with black ice, thick
drifted snow.

Remember to drive slowly given what brief daylight
must remain.

Recall one breath or curve, one echo or chime, quick
bright release

from tentative, awkward moments before the storm.
Rest your warm

exquisite hands on both gray pillows, as white
bed sheets tremble. One

scent. Jasmine. This room lit pale blue—
each bamboo shade drawn.

The Magician Who Lives One Flight Above

He hurries across our cobblestone alley, away
from sleet, morning fog, bundled in scarves, hidden

under his black umbrella, stops in the tailor's doorway, sips
coffee, twirls a cigarette between his slender fingers, weighing

whether to light it, or not, his face obscured
by a red fedora.

This day is trembling
with nervous promise of abundant misdirection, as now

in reliable stone-gray sky
I discover a brilliant violet bruise.

Before the Deluge

Calico cat
bathed in white

moonlight
on my window sill

peers at each
hard curve in the road

poised for all
inevitable commotion

Beneath the Queen Elizabeth Hotel

Time has vacated this metro platform far below
our whispering room.

You linger near the glowing tracks, your face
a shadow in humid light

sure to disconnect, when a rumbling echo
ripples in the black maw

of the enticing tunnel. I will not
write you as one pulse

falling, leaning into nothing.

When You Wake After a Storm

Every shadow is a slim ghost in your dimly
lit lamplight. You cannot return
to sleep, instead light a cigarette
found in that secret gold case you keep

under all your heavy as day manuscripts
askew on your bedside table. You rise, cover
your shoulders with the pale
blue robe, drift close to the bay window, pause

while you listen for what by now
must be no more than distant
thunder. Only one reverie will find its way
to you on steel gray mist, consume

all remaining dark hours before
morning, when you will feel close to safe
within all your hectic work
over another long day of ash gray

rain, blistering wind, in this faithless
season of endless rain.

In the Summer Afternoon Sky

Azurite clouds. Thick rain will not drown
the stone garden, lush
in its own heat. The soaked
air now bathes my wall slick. Blue
light feathers across the bed. Jasmine tea
steeps in a yunomi
cup. I sit and breathe.
Each in breath
deep, each
out breath
slow. Each present

moment a wonderful
moment. The one
white pillow
beside me will fray
over time, yet
in its imperfection will
remain a pillow. The yunomi
cup may chip, but will
remain a cup.

Elderly

While finishing a second cup of coffee
on another humid, overcast morning
I can, with ease, imagine
Big Sur, finding an old blue house
with a view of lush waves, a hazy
on and on.   I must admit
I've never been to Big Sur.
    I must admit I've become
somewhat of a recluse. If I venture
outdoors again, I hope
to come upon Bobo Hydrangeas
to pluck from a neighbor's garden.
    Months ago, my dentist called me elderly
during some on and on about decay. I remember
being aware elderly was useless
to deny by mathematics or discourse.
    My dentist is skillful, thorough, intent
on having her patients experience
little or no pain.   My dentist is optimistic.
I want to believe she will inevitably
lean toward Camus who wrote, "We need the sweet
pain of anticipation to tell us we are really alive."
    Once I requested a red-tail hawk sticker
my dentist gives to children.   She gave me three.
    When she said "elderly," perhaps
I whispered "Elderly? No way." Her response—
"Sorry, you're wrong."   The exam
went on. Pain minimal. I intend to attempt
no denial in the future.   A feeble
rain is falling. Time for more coffee.
Big Sur remains
oh so pleasantly elusive.

The Field of All Possibilities

Painting by Ken Dubin, Fairfield, Iowa
The Field of All Possibility

It is September, let's believe it's one September
night at a gallery, and I'm enticed
      by *The Field of all Possibility.* In time fixed,

      implied, I've avoided any glide to another, a next
painting by what appears, as this surface
      turns liquid, and let's believe, just below this teasing

      surface, an image is forming, formed in the painter's
imagination at some past time, intended
      to detain me in this weightless crowd, conversing

      between sips of white wine, bites of cubed cheese,
but no one nudges me, no one leans
      into me, trying to move me along, to find some thick

      stroke or color more enticing in the next painting, no
derivative comments, knowing looks,
      let's believe, meant to shift my attention to the next

      painting, perhaps the one after, until I've lost
and forgotten *The Field of all Possibility*
      and its troubling, engrossing image always forming

      just below its calm surface, if, let's believe, an image
must be forming, was formed, and this surface,
      in this now dissolving crowd, is truly, deeply calm.

The Cricket

There is a cricket hidden near our blue door
under our juniper hedge
A sign of autumn in Japan the bell cricket is a symbol

of good fortune vitality prosperity and much
admired for its singing
made by its wings and body vibrations

In Kyoto you will find Bell Cricket Temple
where they raise crickets
so people can meditate to each unique song

We discovered the bell cricket can also
represent a unique woman

I don't know what kind of cricket sings
outside our home but we refuse to imagine
chasing this cricket away

in any way interfering with its song

Again in Autumn

Woodsmoke scent Freya. I cannot resist
wondering if you still live

in Montreal content with the harsh
winters, long, yet suitable.

I cannot help wanting you living pacific—
Carmel or Kyoto.

But now a chill breeze roils gold and red
leaves, gentles me back

to the kitchen, where I might come close
to forgetting, refuse

any wistful conjuring of these staggering
years. I want a reverie—

you living anywhere you have whispered,
here will be fine, this

will do quite well, and you can embrace
all that will come next.

Autumn Morning

One imaginary gull hovers
above invisible, hushed waves
that lick our lee shore. Heat can't slice

a thick mist, burn narrow
cobblestone lanes. Opaque shades
are drawn in this town's one small café.

A twisting, slick road
will only breach, dissolve
along each jagged, inarticulate cliff.

The Garden of Kyoto

In this dream I tend one garden at dusk
I'm a monk   I'm old

yet not too weary of work   still relish
night's tender reward

all such pleasures of ease calm release pause
mingle in this dream

with each pale moment

Elm Trees

One September I lingered in a town
with no intention
to stay. Twilight clung
to any warm breeze. On narrow streets
there were regal old houses in need of repair.

Elm trees lined the narrow
sidewalks, their heavy limbs bare,
each trunk's decaying girth
marked with a slash of white paint, one
crooked, careless X
warning of Dutch elm disease.

    I waited for a job; the elms
waited for nothing
but to be cut down.   Every day
there was a shrill of chain saws.
    At times that shrill
must have been no more
than a faint unease, a faint
whisper of failure, of falling, of absence.

Rain

Rough wind off Lake Champlain and rain
visible in Vermont, while here
on the New York shore, rain
is a scent in the chill,
damp air seeping
through one open window. Last night
there was frost. The crisp
painted leaves had been flaring,
vibrant, since late September.
Now I doubt any clean, true
October wash of color
will linger, if rain
cuts the bright leaves loose
on the wind, leaving
all the branches bare. The pandemic
will remain, flu season
must arrive as always, and winter
sleet will likely come
early, a prelude of greasy roads.
There was a harvest moon last night,
ice-white, a dapple of crystals
sparkling on the quiet lake.
Yet now rain
today, again tomorrow. Rain
biting hard at a slant,
soaking the grass and roiling
down the storm pipes.
Waves foam as Vermont dissolves
within a deep mist. The rain
hisses, slaps every window
in its now inevitable, relentless way.

The Beach House in Autumn

Gloucester, Massachusetts, The North Cape

Early morning and taut wind lathers curling waves, chills
empty dunes and beach, a seawall railing. This house
is white with red shutters, likely empty
since early September.   Today will be slate, another
weary hint of winter.   There's a loft, high windows
wet with mist, one large rolltop desk, what must
be oak shelves rising on white walls
heavy under the weight of books.   Facing the Atlantic
a large red door, white stone steps,
a patch of lawn. Close to the seawall path
one granite bench is beckoning
anyone to rest one moment, read the tribute
carved for a son taken by AIDS in 1986.
    For one or many reasons that will always be unknown
to those wandering by, someone
has nailed a For Sale sign to the door, jittery
black letters on white-washed cardboard.   Does it imply
giving up, giving in, despair or relief?   The truth
as Oscar Wilde once wrote is rarely
pure and never simple.
    You could allow any reverie to spin out, take
one form, another, then one more.
For now it might be best to ease down
on the bench, stare out
at endless gray sky now threatening rain.
    Behind you always the red door, rolltop desk,
thick library of books, that might
suggest a soothing truth. How not
to spoil any simmering reverie.

C.W. Pencil Enterprise

15 Orchid Street, New York City

My Blackwing, Malin, and Figueira pencils arrive
early this morning. I will sharpen
the graphite, shape the wood, admire one
especially unique ferrule. Revising a poem, first draft
to last, I use pencil, never bruise a page
with ink. I know my limits.   I always have doubt.
Revision after revision is my intent, always
aware perfection is impossible, despite
any ardent labor. I try to keep
Sisyphus in mind.   Stronger than his stone.

Later this morning I'll put aside my latest
draft. Let it rest. Return to it
tomorrow. I'll wait to order
six Shanghai "Chung-Hwa," one more Tombow.
    I'm in no hurry.

About the Author

Michael Carrino holds an M.F.A. in Writing from Vermont College of Fine Arts. He is a retired English lecturer at the State University College at Plattsburgh, New York, where he was a co-founder and poetry editor of the *Saranac Review.* His previously published books are: *Some Rescues, Under This Combustible Sky, Café Sonata, Autumn's Return to the Maple Pavilion, By Available Light, Always Close, Forever Careless,* and *Until I've Forgotten, Until I'm Stunned,* as well as individual poems in numerous journals and reviews.

www.ingramcontent.com/pod-product-compliance
Lightning Source LLC
Chambersburg PA
CBHW071752090426
42738CB00011B/2657